Original title:
Whispers of the Island

Copyright © 2025 Creative Arts Management OÜ
All rights reserved.

Author: Helena Marchant
ISBN HARDBACK: 978-1-80581-651-5
ISBN PAPERBACK: 978-1-80581-178-7
ISBN EBOOK: 978-1-80581-651-5

Murmurs Over the Tide

A crab in a coat spins around,
While seashells gossip without a sound.
The fish in the sea giggle and play,
As the sun dips low at the end of the day.

Seagulls swoop in, looking for snacks,
One swipes a sandwich, oh, what a lax!
The tide rolls in, with waves that tease,
As pelicans dance, doing the limbo with ease.

Shadows Dancing on the Shore

Beach umbrellas sway like dancers, oh my,
While tourists attempt a graceful sky-high.
Sandcastles crumble in comical falls,
As the moon laughs softly and night gently calls.

Footprints emerge, then vanish like dreams,
Left by a dog chasing after its beams.
The shells crack jokes, each with a punch,
As tidepools erupt in a bubbly munch.

Songs of the Forgotten Cove

In a cove where mermaids may once have swum,
An octopus juggles with soft sea foam gum.
Clams sing tunes out of key but loud,
While dolphins flip, showcasing their crowd.

An old whale hums tales from the deep,
As starfish tap dance on rocks that do leap.
Seas everywhere wave their hands in delight,
In a foamy fiesta that lasts through the night.

Breezes Carrying Memories

The wind tells tales of silly old gnomes,
Who built tiny homes from seashells and foam.
It tickles the sand and shakes the palm trees,
Making the locals giggle with ease.

Kites fly high, tangled in a wild chase,
While laughter erupts, it's a joyful embrace.
A beach ball bounces, a playful retreat,
As the day rolls on with a rhythmic beat.

Desires Carried in the Foam

The sea had dreams of a dapper crab,
With a top hat and cane, oh what a flab!
He danced on the shore, all decked out in flair,
Then slipped on a wave, now he's stuck in mid-air.

Oysters giggled at his rubbery plight,
A seagull swooped down, caught a glimpse of the sight.
"You're quite the bold gent, dear crustacean so spry!",
While the fish trade secrets with a wink of an eye.

Secrets Etched in Driftwood

A piece of driftwood, with stories to tell,
Of pirate's gold buried—oh, wouldn't that sell?
But instead it just hosts a conference of bugs,
Who debate over crumbs and exchange little hugs.

'The last time a hand tried to touch this fine wood,
It splintered and shouted, 'I'd rather feel good!'
They chuckled, then danced as the tide rolled on in,
Feeling blessed for the laughter, not caring to win.

You Can Hear the Horizon Sing

The horizon croons tunes from a leaky shell,
While starfish form bands, oh they play so well.
A clam joins the chorus with a treble so bright,
And a lazy old turtle hums bass with delight.

But what of the gull perched high on the rocks?
She squawks out the rhythm, adds beats just like socks!
The waves clap along in a foam-filled ballet,
While the sun rolls its eyes at this musical fray.

The Allure of Abandoned Coves

In a cove where crabs play tag,
I found a flip-flop, not a rag.
It waved to me, so lost yet proud,
Said, 'Join the party, it's quite loud!'

Seashells dig in, some sing an ode,
Traveling turtles called it home mode.
Seagulls laugh as they steal my fries,
Who knew a bird could wear such ties?

Dreams Carried by the Trade Winds

The breeze nudges my sunburned nose,
I'm chasing shadows left by toes.
A crab in shades with snacks to share,
Claims the beach looks better in a chair.

Palm trees sway to a salsa beat,
As I try to dance—they think I cheat.
With coconuts just hanging around,
Who knew they'd be so tightly bound?

Lanterns of the Night Sky

Stars twinkle like they're playing tag,
While I trip over my own rag.
The moon is laughing, oh what a sight,
Reminds me of my last failed kite flight.

A glow-worm offers light for my snack,
Said, 'Don't eat it! It won't come back!'
Fireflies join—a flash mob, no fear,
I just hope they don't show up in beer.

Revelations Beneath Canopy Leaves

Under leaves where giggles hide,
A squirrel's gossip can't abide.
"Did you hear he'd traded his nuts?"
"Ha! For acorns? That's just nuts!"

Frogs croak out a late-night tale,
While butterflies decide to bail.
Each blossom blushes in the joke,
Soon a sleepy sloth will stoke.

Threading Stars in the Ocean's Fabric

The stars above are fishy friends,
They twinkle bright, where the sea bends.
In jellyfish suits, they dance and prance,
"Who's that?" you ask, "Just the ocean's chance!"

The moon throws a party, waves do a jig,
With clams on the floor, it's quite the gig.
A crab in a tux, looking so elite,
Says, "Keep it quiet, we can't miss this beat!"

The Pulse of the Ocean Heart

The ocean's heart beats strong and loud,
A whale's snore wraps the ocean crowd.
Fish form a band, with bubbles and glee,
   Playing underwater songs, carefree!

"Hey Octopus, play me a tune!"
He strums on a seahorse, under the moon.
The jellybeans jam, they bounce with flair,
   While turtles groove without a care!

Lull in the Sound of Nature

Silence falls, like a wet sock,
Then a clam sneezes, what a shock!
A crab whispers jokes, in its own silly way,
"Lobster told a joke, but it got away!"

The breeze tickles the trees and the sand,
While seabirds squawk in a strange band.
They harmonize while chasing flies,
Under the sun, they make us cry!

Solace Found in Seafoam Trails

In the seafoam lies a laugh or two,
A starfish smiles, saying, "How do you do?"
The sandcastles giggle with silly pride,
As tides come crashing, they try to hide.

Seagulls play catch with a floating fry,
While turtles debate, "Should we fly?"
Under the sun, life's a delightful sleight,
With ocean's jokes, it's all pure delight!

The Gentle Call of Distant Horizons

The gulls in the sky, they squabble and shout,
With laughter as waves play hide and seek about.
Secrets are shared with the shells on the shore,
Each tide brings a giggle, a want for some more.

A hammock hangs low, swaying soft and slow,
While sunbathers giggle, turning bright like a glow.
Crabs dance on the sand, with a shimmy and sway,
Paddling in puddles, just wasting the day.

Serenade of the Sea Breeze

The breeze tells a tale, its voice smooth as cream,
Tickling our noses, a mischievous dream.
Palm trees are swaying, in tune with the fun,
While starfish debate who gets iced in the sun.

Seagulls in sunglasses perform on the edge,
While turtles do the cha-cha, a swaying pledge.
Each wave brings a chuckle, a splashy encore,
The sandy dance floor, who could ask for more?

Dreams of Coral and Conch

In the depths of the sea, where fish wear a grin,
A conch shells a tune that gets under your skin.
The coral's bright colors play tricks on the eye,
While octopuses twirl, oh look at them fly!

Starfish pool parties beneath sparkling light,
With cocktails of seaweed, it's quite a delight.
The laughter of dolphins breaks through the surprise,
As they leap and they twist, with joy in their eyes.

Shadows Beneath the Banyan

The banyan tree whispers, its roots like a joke,
Playing hide and seek with each curious folk.
Lizards hold court, in a sun-drenched debate,
While monkeys concoct plans that just can't wait.

Each leaf sings a tune, quite silly indeed,
A comedy show where the insects all lead.
As shadows grow long, and the sun starts to wane,
We laugh with the breeze, life's a sweet refrain.

Cradled by the Breezy Dawn

A seagull stole my breakfast roll,
I chased it down, what a goofy stroll!
The sun peeked out, a golden gleam,
I tripped on sand, fell right on my dream.

The waves giggled, splashing my face,
Crabs danced by in a silly race.
I laughed so hard, I nearly cried,
As beach balls flew like balloons untied.

Echoing Secrets of the Past

An old flip-flop told me a tale,
Of fishy friends and a bouncy whale.
I joined the chat, with seaweed snacks,
While hermit crabs plotted sneaky attacks.

Conch shells sang songs of yesteryear,
While waves clapped hands, full of cheer.
The sun's a jester, bright and bold,
Its laughter echoes, never gets old.

Murmurs Beneath Ancient Mangroves

The roots twist like pretzels, what a sight,
As frogs perform their froggy night flight.
A raccoon juggled berries with flair,
While the owls giggled, despite the scare.

Bugs shared jokes, with tiny grins,
As lizards played cards, winks and spins.
I sipped some juice, but it turned sour,
The ants threw a party at the top of the tower.

Dancing Shadows Under the Canopy

Trees salsa while the breezes sway,
Their branches join in a playful ballet.
Squirrels crisp their fur, take a chance,
As sunbeams shine, they start to prance.

A little chipmunk brought a snack,
With acorn hats, a colorful pack.
The shadows giggled, shifting about,
In nature's dance, there's never a doubt.

Serenading the Golden Sands

Beneath the sun, the crabs all dance,
They pinch my toes, while I glance.
The seagulls squawk, a feathery choir,
As I sip my drink, my feet in the fire.

A flip-flop flies, a beach ball bounces,
Kids build castles, while sunscreen pounces.
The tide rolls in, and oh what a mess,
I slip on wet sand, in my best sundress.

The beach umbrella spins like a top,
Chasing my snacks, making me stop.
With laughter and giggles in the salty air,
We can't keep up with the seagulls' flair.

As sunset arrives, we toast with our drinks,
Sharing wild stories and playful winks.
Here's to the laughter, the fun that we share,
On these golden sands, with not a single care.

Whims of the Wind's Embrace

The breeze plays tricks, it lifts my hat,
Swirls it away, just like that!
I chase it down, feet flying fleet,
While my friends all laugh, they can't take heat.

A kite in the sky, flying high and wide,
But my snack flies too, what a bumpy ride!
Waves start to giggle, in frothy delight,
As I wrestle my towel, what a funny sight!

The palm trees sway, with a rhythm so clear,
Dancing along to a beat we all cheer.
Nature's own band, they play on repeat,
While we bop to the sound, feeling light on our feet.

Under the moonlight, we share our tales,
Of lost flip-flops and gusty gales.
With laughter around, it feels like a song,
Our hearts in the breeze, where we all belong.

The Soul of the Vibrant Coast

The surfboards tumble, like pups at play,
One nose-dives under, oh what a fray!
Beach balls collide, like a chaotic fling,
As laughter erupts, we all start to sing.

Mermaids in dreams, with sun-kissed skin,
Writing our names, let the fun begin!
The ocean grins, with bubbles galore,
It swirls up our laughter, and asks for more.

Dancing in sand, we form silly shapes,
With a side of sunburn, as laughter escapes.
The dolphins jump, giving us a show,
As we slip on wet rocks, it's a wild flow!

With bright laughter echoing into the night,
Cargo shorts flapping, what a silly sight!
The coast hugs us close, in a glow of cheer,
As we share funny stories, with friends so dear.

Notes of Calm in a Turbulent Sea

The waves crash loud, like pets gone wild,
My beach chair toppled, I feel like a child.
With snacks airborne, oh where do they land?
I chase after chips, with laughter so grand.

Sunblock battles, I squirt in a swirl,
It's a slip 'n' slide, my favorite whirl.
Seashells giggle, in shades so bright,
While I trip on my towel, oh what a sight!

Salty sea breezes whisper and tease,
As I shake off the sand, all sticky like cheese.
The surf sings a tune, with a tickle and jest,
Making sandcastles burst, oh what a fest!

When twilight descends, with stars up high,
We reminisce, as the ocean sighs.
With giggles and grins, in this fun little spree,
Here's to our laughter, forever carefree.

Enchantments at Dusk

The crabs held a dance, they swayed to the tune,
While seagulls squawked loudly, insisting it's noon.
A coconut fell with a bang on my head,
I laughed with the parrot, who just winked instead.

The stars started winking, they aimed for my snack,
I kept them at bay with a strong coconut crack.
The tide tickled toes, made a splash on my shoe,
I yelled at the ocean, 'Hey, I'm not through!'

Litanies of the Sea Breeze

The breeze told a secret, I leaned in so near,
It laughed at my wig, taking flight like a deer.
I chased down a dolphin, said, 'Let's have a race!'
He flipped with a giggle, made me feel like a ace.

The waves started singing a tune of their own,
In a language of bubbles, my giggles were grown.
A starfish was nodding, he quite liked my style,
With sunglasses and sunscreen, he showed off his smile.

Phantoms Beyond the Reef

The fish threw a party, with glittery scales,
They boogied and jived, ignored all my wails.
I joined in the fun, was a sight to behold,
In a grass skirt made of seaweed, bright and bold.

The octopus winked, said he'd teach me his moves,
But tangled my feet in his long stretchy grooves.
I tripped on a clam, fell into their scene,
They cheered and they howled, I was crowned the marine!

Chants of the Gentle Current

The current was playful, it tickled my toes,
Inviting me onward, in jiggles and prose.
A turtle in glasses said, 'Let's race away!'
I hopped on his shell, we were off for the day.

With jellyfish friends, we formed quite a crew,
In a conga line groove, what a sight to pursue!
The sun took a bow as we laughed with the tide,
In our watery world, we let humor be our guide.

Voices of the Turquoise Depths

In the sea, the fish have jokes,
Clowning around with silly strokes.
Octopus spins its best tall tale,
While tiny shrimp dance without fail.

Gulls caw loudly, claiming the sky,
While crabs waddle, oh so spry.
The turtle grins, it knows the scoop,
As dolphins join the giddy group.

Anemones wave with glee,
While seaweed sways like a marquee.
Starfish giggle, stuck in their spot,
Reminding all, life's a funny plot.

Coral reefs hum a merry tune,
While sea cucumbers sway like a balloon.
In turquoise depths, laughter is found,
Among the creatures, joy knows no bound.

Echoing Through the Mangroves

In tangled trees, the monkeys play,
Swinging and laughing all the day.
Their chatter echoes, a playful sound,
As if the forest's laughter is profound.

Crabs play tag, with shells that gleam,
While lizards sunbathe, living the dream.
A heron chuckles, lost in the spray,
As frogs croak puns in a jovial way.

The breeze carries tales of the might,
Of fireflies prancing in the night.
Each leaf whispers with a giggling tease,
While branches bob gently, riding the breeze.

In this green world, humor is king,
Where nature's creatures forever cling.
The mangroves vibrate with life's banter,
As every critter becomes a dancer.

The Heartbeat of the Island's Soul

The palm trees sway with dance so grand,
Chiming like bells in a quirky band.
Flowers gossip with colors bright,
As hibiscus grins in the warm sunlight.

The sunbathers lounge, hats askew,
Telling tall tales—who knows what's true?
Seagulls squawk with comedic flair,
Sharing secrets floating in the air.

Kites soar high, with colors ablaze,
While children giggle in a sunny haze.
The rhythm of laughter fills the coast,
As waves join in, sounding like a boast.

On the shore, sandcastles compete,
With quirky designs, a playful feat.
Each grain of sand holds a tale to spin,
Of the island's heart, where mirth begins.

Nature's Sonnet of Serenity

The breeze teases flowers, they giggle and sway,
While bees buzz in rhythms, sweeting their play.
A sleepy koala hangs with grace,
Winking at nature's fun-loving face.

A butterfly flutters, a prankster it seems,
Painting the air with whimsical dreams.
The sun peeks through leaves, a cheeky grin,
As squirrels chitter, let the games begin!

Rain clouds gather, poke fun at the sun,
While puddles splash—and now the fun's begun!
Nature's laughter in every rustle and cheer,
Echoes of joy, ringing crystal clear.

Serenity hums in a lighthearted song,
Where creatures and critters all dance along.
In this cradle of life, where smiles bloom wide,
The humor of nature is where we confide.

Sentinels of the Moonlit Shore

By the rocks, the crabs do dance,
In moonlight's glow, they take their chance.
With tiny claws, they move around,
While seagulls laugh without a sound.

A starfish tells a sly old tale,
Of fish who tried to catch a whale.
But all they caught was seaweed's grip,
And now they dream of a better trip.

The moonbeams flicker on the tide,
As turtles wear a goofy stride.
With shells like hats, they march in line,
And wave goodnight to the ocean's shine.

So if you stroll the beach at night,
You'll find the tricks of bumpy flight.
For every grain of sand holds glee,
A secret joke for you and me.

The Rhythm of the Gentle Rain

Pitter-patter on the ground,
The frogs start leaping all around.
With slicked-back hair and tiny ties,
They hold a dance beneath the skies.

The raindrops tickle all the birds,
They sing of worms in silly words.
With every splash, they look at you,
A soggy song that's far from blue.

The puddles turn to tiny pools,
Where turtles play the silliest fools.
They spin and twirl, with joy they glide,
While ducks just watch, eyes open wide.

As lightning draws a silly face,
The raindrops dance in a jovial race.
And if you laugh, the clouds will cheer,
For every giggle, the rain draws near.

Ancestral Chants of the Coastal Breeze

The wind brings tales from days of yore,
With whispers of pirates on the shore.
Through swaying palms, a sighing tune,
As coconuts tumble, oh what a boon!

Sea gulls gossip, feathers fluffed high,
About a clam with dreams to fly.
He wears a shell that glimmers bright,
And claims to soar by morning light.

A breeze blows laughter to the trees,
Where chattering monkeys tease the bees.
With every swing and goofy fling,
They challenge crabs to a silly thing.

And in the twilight, stars will wink,
As tides pull in with a playful blink.
For every gust, a grin is cast,
Ancestral jokes that ever last.

Legends Concealed in Coral Reefs

Beneath the waves, a turtle sips,
As fish perform their acrobatic flips.
A clownfish winks in colors bold,
Claiming treasures worth their weight in gold.

The octopus spins a yarn so grand,
With eight slim arms, he takes a stand.
"Where's my treasure?!" he cries in jest,
As shrimps join in, they're quite the best!

The seaweed flags wave stories true,
Of sailors' pranks and fish that flew.
While neighbors clash in a playful fight,
Their laughter echoes through the night.

So dive right in, the tales are sweet,
With every reef, a funny feat.
For legends hold a cheeky flair,
And sea life knows just how to share.

The Language of the Seashells

In a little shell, I found a snail,
It told me jokes, without fail.
Each laugh a bubble, each giggle a wave,
Who knew sea critters could be so brave?

I asked the crab about his dance,
He clicked his claws, gave me a chance.
With a wiggle and a jig, we made quite a show,
Even the fish swam up to the flow!

The starfish chimed in with a starry wink,
He pondered life while sipping a drink.
"Why walk on sand? It's really quite bland,
Just float with your friends in the shifting strand!"

So here we gather, in salty delight,
Telling our tales till the end of the night.
Through giggles and gurgles, we fill up the sea,
In the shell's secret language, oh joyous and free!

Luminous Tales of the Twilight Cove

In twilight's glow, the stories rise,
From glowworms flickering, oh what a surprise!
A shark in a bow tie shared satire and jokes,
While turtles chuckled in their green, cozy cloaks.

A lanternfish shined, showing off his style,
"I'll light the way, just stay for a while!"
They feasted on plankton, a banquet supreme,
As seahorses pranced, fulfilling their dream.

Tides rolled in with a comical rush,
While otters played tag in a frothy hush.
"Catch me if you can!" they merrily sang,
While dolphins spun circles with a joyful twang.

As night draped calm, the cove came alive,
With stories of joy where all creatures thrive.
In laughter and light, we found our true home—
In the glow of the dark, we will always roam!

Sighs from the Shimmering Lagoon

In the lagoon, the lily pads float,
While frogs in tuxedos sing, take note!
The catfish, a bard, recites quite a tale,
Of the time he chased a snail on a rail!

A parrot fish squawked, "I can do it too!"
He painted his scales in a wild hue.
With a whirl and a twirl, he dazzled the crowd,
While the eels whispered softly, "Aren't we so proud?"

A crab hosted bingo, all in good cheer,
"Don't be a fool, just stick close, my dear!
Let's win some pearls and trade them for glee,
And dance 'til the dawn in our watery spree!"

The night dripped with laughter, tidal and bright,
As fish shared their fables until morning light.
With giggles and splashes, oh what a song—
In the lagoon's shimmer, we all belong!

Breath of the Misty Dawn

In misty dawn, the sun peeks through,
A squirrel in a hammock waves, "Hey, how do you do?"
The monkeys are swinging with a chuckle and cheer,
Making breakfast jokes as they near and endear.

Crabs in pajamas scuttled for fun,
"Let's make pancakes with shells!" they yelled, "Let's run!"
While the roosters performed in their plumed best,
The island's a stage, we've passed every test.

The breeze tickles noses, all waking with flair,
As geckos recite poetry from the air.
"Forests feel funny at such an hour,
Where laughter and roots intertwine with power!"

In the day's first glow, we toast with a cheer,
To the wonders of mornings that sparkle and steer.
With each little giggle, we greet the sun's grace,
In the breath of the dawn, we all find our place!

The Melodies of the Distant Horizon

Seagulls gossip in the breeze,
Crabs dance all around with ease.
A whale's tune drifts from afar,
   Promising tales of a jelly star.

The sun wears shades, a funky sight,
While dolphins leap with pure delight.
A coconut drops, missed by a chap,
Who swears he saw a treasure map.

Bananas sing, in pots they stew,
Each fruit a jest, as they pursue.
An octopus juggles seashells bright,
As beachgoers cheer, what a funny sight!

And crabs exchange funny puns,
They challenge each other, just for fun.
Underneath the azure hue,
Laughter reigns, it's all so true!

Ballad of the Lost Fisherman

Old Joe thought he'd snag a whale,
But found instead a soggy pail.
He set his net with grand intent,
And caught a shoe, with no lament.

His boat was named the 'Sea-Serious',
But fish found it quite mysterious.
With every cast, he'd start to grin,
For every catch was full of spin.

A fish with glasses winks with glee,
"Good luck, my friend, you're funny to see!"
He tossed his lines as if in dance,
While fish giggled at his chance.

The tide rolled in with a teasing tone,
Fishermen laughed till they felt like home.
Though Joe went out to catch a feast,
He came back with tales, at least!

Echoes of Solitude

In a hammock, dreams do sway,
A crab plays chess, 'tis quite the play.
While coconuts roll with a laugh,
Lost in the fun, forget the path.

The lone parrot tells a joke,
As the waves crash, and the fish croak.
A starfish reads a novel bold,
About a pirate who lost his gold.

A sunset's blush throws colors bright,
As seagulls join in the silly flight.
Moon whispers secrets on the shore,
While laughter echoes, asking for more.

So here we sing in quiet fun,
With stories twinkling under the sun.
For solitude, a raucous game,
Not a dull moment, that's the aim!

Secrets Beneath the Palm

Beneath the palm, a party brews,
With fruit hats on, the locals muse.
A turtle tells of days of yore,
When he outran a chasing shore.

The breeze reveals a silly song,
Bees buzz along, they hum along.
A shrimp with style, he steals the show,
In shades of pink, he's quite the pro.

Laughter bounces, a playful chase,
As iguanas dance with style and grace.
The secrets held in the coconuts,
Are tales of pranks and silly guts.

So gather 'round for tales so bright,
Of secrets tangled in the night.
For what lies beneath, we shall not say,
But laughs will linger, come what may!

Conversations with the Surf

The waves they chat, with giggles loud,
They splash on shore, so very proud.
"So many shells!" one says with glee,
"I think I'll start a beachside spree!"

A crab walks by, with sideways strut,
"Could you be quieter? You're in my rut!"
The tide just laughs, it won't relent,
"You're lucky, friend, I'm all but spent!"

A seagull joins, with a cheeky squawk,
"What's all this chatter? Let's take a walk!"
But as they roam, the wind takes sway,
And all their tales are blown away!

With salty jokes and sand-filled sands,
The humor flows like tiny bands.
At dusk they promise to meet again,
For laughter in the moonlit glen.

Tales Carried by the Wind

The breeze began to tell a tale,
Of little fish who dared to sail.
"They thought they'd reach that distant shore,
But ended up by lookin' for more!"

A parrot squawked, he knew it well,
"Those fish were nuts, just look at their shell!"
The wind would howl and bend with glee,
As birds would flit from tree to tree.

A message flew to every ear,
"Take a chance, let go of fear!"
But in the end, the fish were found,
In a lobster pot, all tightly bound!

The wind just laughed, it had its fun,
As tales of folly spun and spun.
With every gust, a new delight,
Brought smiles to all, from morn till night.

Reflections in the Calm Waters

In waters clear, a fish made faces,
Attempting tricks in silly places.
"Just look at me!" it seemed to say,
"I'm quite the star in this ballet!"

A frog hopped by with a wink so sly,
"What's with the splash? Please tell me why!"
The fish just flipped, with all its charm,
"I'm training hard! So stay alarmed!"

The ripples laughed, they danced and played,
Creating stories, all unafraid.
"If only they knew we're just a jest,
In nature's game, where we are blessed!"

At sunset's glow, with skies ablaze,
Both critters basked in giggling phase.
For in this peace, as day did end,
They'd share these laughs, just round the bend.

The Solace of Secluded Cove

In a cove so snug, the crabs convene,
Sharing secrets, a quirky scene.
"Last week I saw a fish in socks!"
They chuckled softly, hiding in rocks.

A starfish chimed in, all aglow,
"I wear my best, don't you know?"
But one crab said, with eyes of cheer,
"That style is great, but don't come near!"

A clam just giggled, plush in its shell,
"You're all absurd, can't you tell?"
While seaweed swayed in playful tease,
The humor grew with every breeze.

As dusk arrived, with laughter grand,
They formed a band with shells in hand.
In that secluded space, so rare,
The joy of friendship danced in air.

Whispers of Gulls in Flight

Gulls hover above, plotting their scheme,
Stealing our fries, like a sly little dream.
With a flap and a squawk, they create such a fuss,
Who knew lunch could turn into gull-ridden bus?

They dive and they dance, like they own the sea,
Making us laugh, it's a comical spree.
Mimicking us as we try to complain,
These feathered jesters bring joy and some bane.

With beaks in the air, they take to the sky,
Chasing each other, you can't help but sigh.
For a sandwich's fate hangs by just a thread,
Thanks to the majesty of birds in our spread.

So, wave to the gulls, let them take their flight,
In their world of mischief, all ends up just right.
Between laughter and crumbs, we find our delight,
Together in chaos, they brighten our sight.

Veils of Mist at Dawn

The morning mist hugs our sleepy retreat,
Where socks on the line all seem to compete.
A foghorn calls out, it sounds quite absurd,
Like a sleepy old man who talks with a slur.

The sun peeks through, with a smirk on its face,
As if to say, 'Time to start this light race!'
In robes of mist, our laughter resounds,
Chasing away slumber, our silliness bounds.

Neighbors arise, in pajamas so bright,
Contemplating breakfast with sleepy delight.
What will it be? Pancakes or maybe a danish?
What a grand debate, oh the choices we banish!

So roll with the fog, let it twirl all around,
As laughter ignites in the soft, misty ground.
With dawn's early light, and our giggles in tow,
We embrace the day's whimsy, wherever it flows.

Reveries of Hidden Shores

On hidden shores where our flip-flops align,
We dig for some treasures, seaweed and brine.
Finding old bottles, we ponder the tales,
Of sailors and pirates and wind in their sails.

A crab scuttles by, with a snippy little jaw,
It's showing off moves that would leave us in awe.
We try to catch it, but he's way too sly,
Like a competitor in this shell-covered tie.

The tide rolls in with a tickle and splash,
As sandcastles melt into a comical mash.
We laugh and we play, as the seagulls convene,
In a sea of good humor, we find our routine.

So dance with the waves, let your joy be the score,
In hidden coves where we always explore.
Every giggle and gig, it's we who restore,
Fun-filled festivities held on the shore.

Stories in the Seashells

Beneath waves of laughter, seashells convene,
Each telling a tale, so quirky and keen.
A conch shell insists, 'I was once a great king!'
In the sands of our imagination, they sing.

A scallop joins in with a wink and a grin,
'I've swum with the dolphins, oh what a win!'
Tinny voices rise from the depths of the bay,
As we sit down to listen, we giggle away.

A tragedy shared by the tattered old shell,
Of being mistaken for a dinner bell.
We chuckle and nod, so grateful to hear,
Each shell holds a secret, a tale we hold dear.

So gather your shells, let your heart swell with glee,
For every little story lets our spirits be free.
With laughter and wonder, we make our own trails,
In the world of the shells, where imagination prevails.

The Treasure of Windswept Isles

The parrot squawks a joke so loud,
As pirates dance and jig, oh proud.
A treasure map on a pizza box,
'X' marks the spot near a pair of socks!

The waves giggle as they lap the shore,
While mermaids' laughter begins to soar.
With shovels made from garden spades,
They dig for gold, but find charades!

Coconut drinks served with silly straws,
The seagulls dive, but give just a pause.
A crab in shades starts strutting around,
On this isle, nonsense knows no bounds!

So come along, join the jesters' fun,
Where sunshine sparkles, and laughter's won.
For buried treasure might not be gold,
But laughter shared, and stories told!

A Symphony of Sunlit Waters

The fish are rehearsing, they hum a tune,
With starfish clapping under the moon.
A dolphin darts through bubbles and foam,
In this watery world, there's no place like home!

The waves tap dance in a rhythmic delight,
As sea turtles waltz, a charming sight.
With flippers flailing and fins a-flap,
They take their bows in a soggy cap!

A playful octopus strums a guitar,
While crabs form a band and sing from afar.
A clam steals the show with its pearl of a joke,
And the seaweed sways as it starts to choke!

Bubbles join in, they float to the beat,
This ocean concert can't be beat.
From sandy shores to coral flares,
Laughter and music fill salty airs!

Captured Moments in Salty Air

A seagull swoops down for a quick selfie,
But ends up tangled in a beach ball, oh golly!
The camera clicks, but it's blurry and bright,
Now that bird is quite the funny sight!

Sandcastles rise, built with such flair,
But watch those waves—they're sneaky with care.
One splash and a tower comes tumbling down,
Leaving kids creased with laughter, no frown!

A clam in a hat rocks the holiday scene,
While starfish fashion a stylish routine.
Sandy feet dance, chasing dreams by the shore,
In moments so silly, who could ask for more?

With kites that get tangled and ice cream that melts,
Each salty excursion just bursts with fun, felt.
These memories linger, forever a flair,
Captured in sunshine, alongside the salty air!

The Elegance of Gentle Currents

The tide rolls in with a smooth ballet,
While jellyfish twirl in the sun's warm ray.
A conch shell whispers secrets with glee,
 'You call this elegant? Look at me!'

Seashells perched like hats on the sand,
With crabs orchestrating a marching band.
A fish in a bow tie swims with style,
While everyone else is just in denial!

Soft breezes tickle, and laughter takes flight,
As sea cucumbers plan for a night out so bright.
In currents that giggle and roll like a joke,
The ocean's a stage, and laughter awoke!

With every ebb, they dance to and fro,
Where elegance hides, but silliness flows.
In playful rhythms, the sea sings along,
Finding joy in a world of whimsical song!

Silken Threads of Nightfall

As the sun dips low, a smirk in sight,
Stars pop out, like popcorn at night.
Sea otters dance with a clumsy grace,
While crabs do the cha-cha in their shell space.

Moonbeams giggle, shining so bright,
Throwing shadows that tickle with delight.
Octopuses juggle their lost treasure,
Making mischief, it's quite the pleasure!

A sandcastle topples, the tide gives a shove,
A crab warns, 'Hey, that's not how we love!'
The night is a stage, the stars are the cast,
In this quirky ballet, time flies by fast!

So gather your friends, let the laughter flow,
For night's just a canvas where wild dreams grow.
With each silly twist and every light cheer,
We'll craft a tale for the waves to hear.

The Art of Listening to the Waves

Ocean murmurs secrets, a bubbly chat,
Telling tales of a fish in a fancy hat.
Seagulls squawk gossip, sharp as a dart,
While the shells play poker, each shell with a heart.

The tide rolls in with a playful nudge,
While the starfish judge, giving a grudge.
'You call that a splash?' one clam says with glee,
As they all convene for a waves' jubilee.

Sand between toes, oh, what a delight!
Where jellyfish waltz under pale moonlight.
Avoiding sea urchins, they dance with finesse,
Turning ocean floors into a grand process.

So lean in closely, hear laughter and glee,
As the waves share stories, so wild and free.
Just keep an ear open, don't miss a giggle,
For Neptune's the DJ; he'll make your toes wiggle.

Tapestry of Light and Water

Threads of sunlight weave through the waves,
Where dolphins play hopscotch, just mischiefy knaves.
A crab tells a tale, one quite absurd,
Of the time it mistook a rock for a bird!

Colors collide as the seagulls squawk,
Painting the sky while the oysters mock.
'You call that a shell?', they giggle and tease,
'At least we don't smell like you, oh, geez!'

Frisky fish flip like they own the show,
While lobsters debate who's the sassiest pro.
A squad of sea cucumbers joins in the mix,
With puns so salty, they'll crack you like sticks.

Twilight drapes over with a wink and a grin,
The sea laughs out loud, it's where fun begins.
So come one, come all, to the watery fun,
In this tapestry bright, we're all on the run!

Lingering Aromas of Sea Grass

The breeze brings snippets of sea grass delight,
Where the fish do the tango, quite out of sight.
Starfish spread rumors while seahorses prance,
All while a sea turtle lost in a trance.

A jellyfish giggles, sassy and free,
Daring each wave to just come and see.
'Catch me if you can!' the little waves say,
As they bubble with laughter, spiralling away.

Sand dollars shuffle, they're planning a race,
While clams throw a party, all in one place.
With bubbles and giggles, the tide rolls in tight,
Creating a show that's sheer sea-sparkling delight.

So taste the sweet scent of sea grass around,
Where laughter blooms freely, joy knows no bound.
Each wave brings a chuckle, a glimmer, a rhyme,
With antics so silly, they'll dance through all time.

Ballads of Sunrise Serenity

The roosters crow with such delight,
As morning joggers take to flight.
A crab scuttles across the lane,
Chasing shadows like it's in a game.

Bikini tops are tangled dread,
While surfers cling to their surfboard's led.
The sun peeks out, a golden coin,
And flip-flops squeak on the beach's join.

Seagulls squawk a morning tune,
While someone's lost their bright maroon.
A floatie bobs in laughter's grace,
Pretending it's a grand embrace.

Oh, how the sun begins to rise,
With funny friends and silly pies.
The island wakes, it's pure delight,
As laughter dances in the light.

The Allure of Glistening Sand

Footprints paint a tale so wild,
Of a sunburnt tourist—just a child.
Sandy toes in flip-flops sway,
Chasing laughter at the sunny bay.

A beach ball flies with all its might,
While sunscreen fights the sun's bright bite.
Umbrellas flutter, hats take flight,
As laughter rings out day and night.

Seashells jingle like a choir,
While kids build castles, never tire.
The sand is sticky with a grin,
As ice cream drips down from their chin.

Oh, what a fun-filled ocean spree,
With joy as vast as the endless sea.
The grainy gems of laughter grand,
That's the charm of glistening sand.

Echoing Footsteps on the Dunes

Footsteps echo like a song,
As someone trips, it won't be long.
The dunes are steep, the climb is tough,
Yet every slip leads to great stuff.

A sandcastle army starts to form,
With knights and kings, a beachy norm.
But watch your step, or you might land,
Face first in wet, glistening sand!

Kites soar high in a tug-of-war,
While someone shouts, "Hey, watch the shore!"
The seashore giggles underfoot,
As laughter springs from every nook.

In these dunes, we jump and play,
Cherishing each absurd, bright day.
Our laughter trails like autumn leaves,
Echoing joy, oh how it weaves!

Reflections of the Setting Sun

The sun descends, a fiery ball,
Marking lunchtime with a brawl.
Chasing sunsets while trying to dine,
As burgers flip—who made that line?

Flip-flops squeak, they're on a spree,
Falling left and right with glee.
A game of frisbee starts to reel,
But someone's dodging with a squeal.

As evening paints the sky in red,
Someone's tangled in a beach blanket spread.
The sounds of laughter fill the air,
While one gets "lost" in a crab's stare.

With each sunset, giggles bloom,
The shore brings joy, it's pure perfume.
Reflections dance as day grows old,
In this funny world, let stories be told.

Reflections in Coral Waters

Fish wearing hats swim around,
They giggle and dance without a sound.
Seashells gossip, tales to unfold,
In the coral, secrets are bold.

A crab in a tux, ready for the ball,
Struts with a swagger, thinking he's tall.
Octopuses juggle with style and grace,
While starfish cheer, all over the place.

A mermaid's laughter fills the air,
As dolphins dive with flair to spare.
Turtles in sunglasses bask and lounge,
While seaweed dancers twirl and bounce.

The sun dips low, painting the sea,
As fish throw a party, wild and free.
Karaoke night, where sea critters shine,
Under the moonlight, oh how they dine!

Lullabies of the Sapphire Sea

Bubbles rise like giggles at night,
As crabs harmonize, everything's bright.
Conch shells whistle soothing tunes,
While jellyfish sway beneath the moons.

A clam sings softly, rocking its bed,
With sea cucumbers nodding their heads.
The sea turtles spin tales of old,
Of treasure hunts and adventures bold.

Seahorses dance in a delicate line,
As fish sing lullabies, feeling divine.
Starry night sparkles with glee,
In the underwater night, so carefree.

Gulls in tuxedos swoop and glide,
Chasing the waves with joyful pride.
All under the sapphire sky so wide,
Laughter and harmony, there's no need to hide.

Tides of Forgotten Dreams

In the sandy shores, dreams play hide,
A sandcastle cowboy has nowhere to ride.
Seashells recall long-lost desires,
As surfboards join aquatic choirs.

The waves clap hands like a cheering crowd,
While starfish strut, feeling proud.
Beach balls giggle as they bounce around,
In this land where joy knows no bound.

An old boat winks, with stories to tell,
Of jellybean sails and a candy shell.
Along comes a seagull, sly and sneaky,
Planning to snag a snack all cheeky.

With every tide, memories wash ashore,
Chasing laughter, always wanting more.
These dreams, forgotten, dance in the foam,
In this whimsical world we call home.

Embraces of the Moonlit Beach

Under the moon, the waves gently sigh,
With seashells dreaming of pizza pie.
Manta rays swoop for a midnight treat,
As sand dances lightly on their feet.

A crab in a scarf tries to impress,
While clowns of the ocean cause silly mess.
Seaweed tickles the toes of delight,
As fish in tuxedos boogie all night.

The moonlight glimmers on playful pranks,
As dolphins gather for cheeky janks.
They spin and they leap, a jubilant show,
In the moon's warm glow, they steal the flow.

Laughter rings out in the soft salty air,
With gulls doing impressions, all unaware.
The night ends with joy, in the bright sands below,
Where the ocean's embrace invites us to grow.

Echoes of Serenity on Quartz Shores

Seagulls gossip with the breeze,
Dancing crabs hold happy tease.
Sandy toes and salty fries,
Beach ball bounces, joy arrives.

Flip-flops flap, a runaway pair,
Chasing tide without a care.
Sunburned noses, laughter bright,
In this paradise, pure delight.

Tanning lotions, scented sweet,
Seashells march with tiny feet.
Coconut drinks in hand we cheer,
Life's a party, feel the cheer!

Merriment lingers like the sun,
Each silly game, a lot of fun.
As evening fades, friends unite,
Under the starry, shining light.

Reflections of the Twilight Mirage

Mirages dance on the sunset sand,
A friendly crab joins the band.
Ice cream spills on a sandy knee,
Who snatched my cup? Not me, not me!

Balloons float in the twilight glow,
Why did my hat just say hello?
Laughter rings as the seagulls sing,
Silly moments that joy will bring.

Funny hats of every shape,
Who wears what? A goofy cape!
Twinkling stars in the sky's embrace,
Paint our smiles in every place.

Jokes are told, and puns arise,
In this twilight, laughter flies.
The night brings friends as shadows blend,
In this mirage, there's never an end.

Hushed Hymns from the Horizon

Turtles slow dance with the waves,
Wily dolphins act like knaves.
Surfboards bumble on the shore,
What a ride! Oh, wait—no more!

Moonlit nights with giggles near,
Sipping drinks and sharing cheer.
Bonfire tales of ghosts and fright,
Who knew they'd end in pure delight?

Sticky marshmallows on our face,
Glimpses of joy in this wild chase.
Bickering friends, but never sore,
Laughter echoes, who could ask for more?

Whispers fly on the ocean breeze,
"Hey, was that a fish?" "Just me, please!"
In this dreamland where joy stays,
The horizon glows with fun-filled rays.

Pathways of Light on Still Waters

Kayaks drift with a splashing cheer,
Frogs leap out, the coast is clear.
Swim trunks ready—oops, wait, fall!
Who knew the lake would call?

Rowboat races, laughter loud,
With silly accents, we feel proud.
A duck parade in a line so neat,
What a sight, can't be beat!

Moonbeams shimmer on the lake,
"Is that a fish?"—or just a wake?
With every quip, the giggles flow,
Paths of light where good vibes grow.

Starry nights bring tales to share,
As we ponder what's up there.
In still waters where laughter shines,
Friendship blooms like intertwining vines.

Tides that Speak in Silence

The ocean laughs, a playful tease,
Saltwater tickles, a cool summer breeze.
Seagulls gossip, wings in a flurry,
Shells gossip secrets—they're never in a hurry.

Crabs hold court, pinching with glee,
Dancing on sand, all wild and free.
The tide pulls back, a coy little dance,
As fish hover close, in a curious trance.

A driftwood throne, for the jester of waves,
Riding the surf, the ocean misbehaves.
Underneath the moon, the silliness flows,
In the splash of foamy laughter, anything goes!

With splashes of humor, a timeless delight,
Cheeky waves giggle, echoing the night.
Each bubble a joke, bursting with fun,
Under the bright and watchful sun.

The Undercurrent's Song

Beneath the surface, the fish all conspire,
With bubbles and giggles, they never tire.
Eels sneak around with a sly little grin,
Snatching the snacks while the crabs just spin.

The octopus juggles, all eight arms in play,
While sea cucumbers crawl, brightening the day.
Every rock holds a secret so bold,
The laughter cascades, richer than gold.

Dolphins dive deep, flip-flopping with cheer,
Delivering punchlines that only they hear.
The currents glimmer with playful intent,
As they twirl and they giggle, all manners of bent.

Tides teasing tales, our jokes set afloat,
In the ripples of fun, we all can remote.
When the horizon blushes, and day bids adieu,
The ocean waves giggle, alive and anew.

Calypso of the Crashing Waves

Oh, the rhythm of tides, a calypso delight,
With splashes and laughter, they dance in the night.
Guitar strumming shells, a melody bright,
While sea stars pirouette, what a wondrous sight!

Crashes and giggles, a symphony grows,
As sandcastles topple like friendly foe throws.
Beachgoers chuckle, with each rising spray,
As fishy comedians come out to play.

The wind carries tunes, the seagrass sways,
Tickling the toes of the sun-warmed bays.
Each wave a chorus, a physical jest,
They sing of the ocean, their bubbly zest.

With driftwood guitars, and shells for the beat,
The party continues—it's quite a treat!
Under the stars, the laughter will bloom,
In the heart of the sea, no hint of gloom.

Mysteries Written in Sand

In the morning light, the sand holds a tale,
Footprints and sketches that can't seem to pale.
Scribbled in flour, a riddle awaits,
As the tide rolls in, it carefully states.

A crab walks the line, a stubborn old chap,
Leaving behind his own little map.
Doodles of dolphins, a fish with a hat,
Creatures of laughter, this humor is that!

Each wave like a laugh, washing jokes on the shore,
In sand, they conspire, each joke to explore.
Signed with a splash, their secrets afloat,
Tickling toes as they softly note.

As evening falls, the tide takes a bow,
Starring the stars, like shells in a row.
The mysteries linger, a sandy buffoon,
Written by water, beneath the bright moon.

Delicate Petals on the Wind

Petals dance like butterflies,
With nothing but a gentle breeze,
They giggle as they soar and spin,
A floral laugh that brings us ease.

Caught in tangled seaweed snags,
They tumble down with silly grace,
Even crabs are chuckling now,
While fish join in the merry race.

The sun plays peek-a-boo today,
As shadows stretch and prance around,
In every twist and every sway,
Laughter's echo is profound.

So let the petals guide our fun,
In nature's jest, we all partake,
With every breeze, a smile begun,
In joyous chaos, we awake.

Finding Solace in Marine Secrets

A clam spoke of its secret heart,
With tales of treasure in the sand,
But when we looked, it flipped apart,
And giggled with a wave-like hand.

A starfish sang of cosmic dreams,
While jellyfish twirled like a boss,
In salty pools, you'd think it seems,
These ocean pals are quite the gloss.

With every splash, a chuckle's shared,
As sea cucumbers throw a fit,
While turtles roll their eyes, unimpaired,
They know it's best to keep a wit.

So dive beneath the frothy waves,
Where laughter lingers, bold and free,
In depths where every creature braves,
The warmth of jubilant, salty glee.

Harmony Beneath the Stars

Stars wink and swirl like dizzy sprites,
Above the waves, a silly scene,
The moon just giggles, what a sight,
As crickets play on seashells keen.

The sand comes alive with shuffles and squeaks,
In this nocturnal, comical play,
Where even the ocean's laughter peaks,
As fish wear hats and dance ballet.

With every tide, the jokes arise,
From dolphins bouncing on a thrill,
They flip, they splash, with gleaming eyes,
And waves applaud with joyous shrill.

So let the dark embrace your cheer,
As constellations spin their tales,
In playful sparkles, laughter near,
In harmony where fun prevails.

Fables of the Tidal Pools

In tidal pools of shining glass,
Tiny creatures weave their yarns,
With tales of clams and fish that pass,
Each story wrapped in frothy barns.

A crab once claimed its throne of sand,
A king adorned with shells and pride,
But fell, then feigned a grand demand,
A court of giggles banked the tide.

The sea anemone told a joke,
About a snail who thought he's swift,
Yet tripped and left a salty smoke,
His slimy trail a clumsy gift.

With every ripple, laughter spreads,
In pools where life and whimsy flow,
These fables dance on soft sea beds,
In nature's joy, a vibrant show.

Silhouettes of Distant Horizons

Palm trees sway in the breeze,
Coconuts drop with a thud,
Seagulls argue with great glee,
Crispy snacks turn to mud.

Sunset paints the sky so bright,
Flip-flops dance in the sand,
Tourists sing with pure delight,
Lost a hat, what a grand plan!

Laughter echoes through the night,
Crabs play tag, what a sight!
A hammock swings, arms flail wide,
Who knew rest could be this try?

In the morning, toast, and jam,
Seashells gather near the shore,
The local cat makes quite a slam,
Steals my lunch, then asks for more!

Tales from the Salt-kissed Coast

A fisherman caught old boots,
Thinking they'd give him fame,
He shared this tale with the brutes,
Now everyone knows his name!

Sandcastles rise with such pride,
Until a wave has its say,
With a splash, they take a ride,
Who knew castles could decay?

The sunburned guys do the dance,
With lotions slathered on thick,
A seagull swoops, gives them a chance,
To show off their elastic trick!

Rum drinks spill in the heat,
Mixing flavors like a chef,
The locals cheer, "What a feat!"
But the blender has no left!

The Language of Shimmering Waves

The waves laugh when the tide rolls in,
A surfer wipes out with a grin,
He says, "I tried my best today,"
But the honor went to the spray!

Seashells sing in the sea foam,
Each is looking for a home,
A starfish waves, "Aren't we grand?"
Sunscreen applied, we hit the strand!

Kids build forts out of driftwood,
Pirates roving, all is good,
Until a wave turns them ashen,
"Avast!" they shout, "We're still fashion!"

A dolphin pops up to check,
"Who's won today, what the heck?"
With a splash, they disappear,
Leaving behind giggles and cheer!

Nuit in the Sunlit Glade

In the glade where sunbeams dance,
Squirrels plotting their next chance,
A raccoon steals a sandwich quick,
Leaving folks all dazed and sick!

Bugs doing cha-cha by the light,
Join the party, oh what a sight!
"Who invited all the flies?"
The picnic blanket's full of sighs!

Fireflies twinkle like glittering dreams,
Bestowing fun on nightly schemes,
Toasting marshmallows, gooey delight,
But someone burned the chocolate right!

They bump into a tree with a thud,
"Next time, let's stay out of the mud,"
As laughter echoes through the trees,
A night to remember in the breeze!

www.ingramcontent.com/pod-product-compliance
Lightning Source LLC
Chambersburg PA
CBHW072122070526
44585CB00016B/1533